x3

An Y0-AEW-222

Sinabouda lily : a folk
tale from Papua New

3 1192 00335 2992

Oxford University Press

OXFORD LONDON GLASGOW
NEW YORK TORONTO MELBOURNE WELLINGTON
NAIROBI DAR ES SALAAM CAPE TOWN
KUALA LUMPUR SINGAPORE JAKARTA HONG KONG TOKYO
DELHI BOMBAY CALCUTTA MADRAS KARACHI

This book is copyright. Apart from any fair dealing for the purposes of private study, research, criticism or review, as permitted under the Copyright Act, no part may be reproduced by any process without written permission. Inquiries should be made to the publishers.

© *Text Robin Anderson 1979*
© *Illustrations Jennifer Allen 1979*

First published 1979

NATIONAL LIBRARY OF AUSTRALIA CATALOGUING IN
PUBLICATION DATA

Anderson, Robin.
  Sinabouda lily.

  For children
  ISBN 0 19 554201 0

  1. Tales, Papua New Guinea — Juvenile Literature.
  I. Allen, Jennifer, illus. II. Title.

  398.21'0995

Distributed in Papua New Guinea
by Robert Brown and Associates Pty Ltd

TYPESET IN 16PT MELIOR BY SGL INDUSTRIES, 582 LITTLE COLLINS STREET, MELBOURNE.
PRINTED IN HONG KONG BY LIANG YU PRINTING FACTORY LIMITED.
PUBLISHED BY OXFORD UNIVERSITY PRESS, 7 BOWEN CRESCENT, MELBOURNE.

'For Richard and David'

EVANSTON PUBLIC LIBRARY
CHILDREN'S DEPARTMENT
1703 ORRINGTON AVENUE
EVANSTON, ILLINOIS 60201

told by
Robin Anderson

pictures by
Jennifer Allen

SINABOUDA LILY

A folk tale from Papua New Guinea

Melbourne
OXFORD UNIVERSITY PRESS
Oxford Wellington New York

On the western side of Kwato Island, in
Papua New Guinea, lived a little girl with
her mother, father and two brothers.
Her name was Sinabouda Lily.

Right beside the water, near their house,
grew a big bodilla nut tree. From one of its
branches hung a loop of thick, green vine.
It made a wonderful swing for the little
girl. People from her village called her
Sinabouda Lily, the swing girl.

Every morning, Sinabouda Lily ran down
to the beach and climbed onto her swing.
Day after day she swung back and forth,
going higher and higher and further and
further, until she almost reached the
nearby island of Bonarurahilihili.

Sinabouda Lily was very happy on her
swing, but her mother warned her, 'You
must be careful, Sinabouda Lily. On the
island of Bonarurahilihili lives the wicked
witch Sinawakelakela Tanotano, and she
loves to eat children!'.

'Oh Mother, I saw the witch yesterday. I told her she couldn't hurt me as long as my father and brothers are here to protect me. But the witch dared me to lean out further, and when I laughed, she shook her fist and said, "One day I will catch you".'

Not long after that, the family had to go
out across the bay on a fishing trip.
Sinabouda Lily begged to be allowed to
stay at home and spend the day on her
swing.

Her mother wasn't happy to leave her, but
her father said she would be quite safe.
He left her a big bunch of ripe bananas over
which he had worked a magic spell.
He told Sinabouda Lily that if she was
frightened, or in any trouble, she had only
to talk to the bananas, and he would hear
her and answer. He hung the bananas on a
branch of the bodilla nut tree.

The rest of the family set out across the
bay in their canoe, leaving Sinabouda Lily
swinging happily back and forth on her
swing. And as she swung, she ate
bananas from the bunch and threw the
skins into the sea.

Sinabouda Lily felt quite safe with the
magic bananas, but her father had
forgotten to tell her one very important
thing. If she ate the bananas and threw
away the skins, the magic spell would not
work.

Across on the island of Bonarurahilihili, the wicked witch Sinawakelakela Tanotano hid and watched as the family set out in their canoe. She crept down to the beach and when she saw the magic banana skins, she rushed to the water's edge to collect them.

High up on her swing, Sinabouda Lily saw the witch collecting the banana skins.

'The wicked witch must be very hungry to collect skins to eat', she thought. And she swung out closer to the island to get a better look.

Suddenly the witch reached out and tried to grab Sinabouda Lily. The little girl screamed, and from the bunch of bananas hanging in the tree came the voice of her father: 'Do not be afraid, my child, I am here'.

When the wicked witch heard the father's voice, she ran away.

Slowly the day passed and the sun was low in the sky.

'Soon my family will return with all their fish', thought Sinabouda Lily. She took the last banana from the bunch and threw the stalk into the sea. Then she climbed back onto her swing to wait for her family to come home. And the banana stalk floated out to sea.

But the wicked witch had been hiding and watching. When she saw Sinabouda Lily eat the last banana and throw the stalk into the sea, she jumped out of her hiding place and grabbed the little girl as she swung out towards the island.

'Ha, ha!', she cried, 'I have caught you at last. I'll soon have you in my cooking pot!'.

Sinabouda Lily screamed, 'Mother! Father!
Brothers!', but it was no use. There was
no answering voice from her father.

The wicked witch tied her up, carried her
along the beach and put her in a cooking
pot.

Far out in the bay, the family saw the
banana stalk floating on the water. They
knew at once that something was wrong
and they quickly turned their canoe and
headed straight for the island of
Bonarurahilihili.

Just as they landed, they saw the wicked
witch struggling up the beach with a load
of firewood for her cooking pot.

She was bent nearly double under the
weight of the wood.

Sinabouda Lily's father rushed at the
witch and struck her down. As she fell
to the ground and died, the firewood
spilled out behind her and she turned into
a rock.

And if you go to that beach on the island
of Bonarurahilihili, near Kwato, you can
still see the rock that is all that remains of
the wicked witch Sinawakelakela
Tanotano.